Envision It! | Visual Skills Handbook

Author's Purpose

Compare and Contrast

Fact and Opinion

Draw Conclusions

Sequence

Literary Elements

EI•1

Author's Purpose

Inform

Entertain

Compare and Contrast

Fact and Opinion

Fact = It is raining.

Opinion = Rainy days are fun!

Draw Conclusions

= Sad

Sequence

Literary Elements

Characters

BROTHER
MOMMY
THE WOLF
DADDY
SISTER

Setting

Plot

Beginning

Middle

End

Envision It! | Visual Strategies Handbook

Background Knowledge

Important Ideas

Inferring

Monitor and Clarify

Predict and Set Purpose

Questioning

Story Structure

Summarize

Text Structure

Visualize

Background Knowledge

Let's **Think** About **Reading!**

- What do I already know?
- What does this remind me of?

Let's **Think** About **Reading!**

- What is important to know?

Inferring

Monitor and Clarify

Let's Think About Reading!

- What does not make sense?
- How can I fix it?

Predict and Set Purpose

Trains

Let's Think About Reading!

- What do I already know?
- What do I think will happen?
- What is my purpose for reading?

Questioning

Let's **Think** About **Reading!**

- What questions do I have about what I am reading?

Story Structure

Beginning

Middle

End

Let's Think About Reading!

- What happens in the beginning?
- What happens in the middle?
- What happens in the end?

Summarize

The dog knocked over the table.

Let's **Think** About **Reading!**

- What happens in the story?
- What is the story mainly about?

Text Structure

Let's **Think** About **Reading!**

- How is the story organized?
- Are there any patterns?

Visualize

Let's **Think** About **Reading!**

- What pictures do I see in my mind?

SCOTT FORESMAN
READING STREET

GRADE 1

COMMON CORE ©

Program Authors

Peter Afflerbach

Camille Blachowicz

Candy Dawson Boyd

Elena Izquierdo

Connie Juel

Edward Kame'enui

Donald Leu

Jeanne R. Paratore

P. David Pearson

Sam Sebesta

Deborah Simmons

Susan Watts Taffe

Alfred Tatum

Sharon Vaughn

Karen Kring Wixson

Glenview, Illinois

Boston, Massachusetts

Chandler, Arizona

Upper Saddle River, New Jersey

ALWAYS LEARNING

PEARSON

We dedicate Reading Street to
Peter Jovanovich.

His wisdom, courage,
and passion for education
are an inspiration to us all.

Accelerated Reader®

Acknowledgments appear on page 230, which constitutes an extension of this copyright page.

ISBN-13: 978-0-328-72446-8
ISBN-10:   0-328-72446-7
5 6 7 8 9 10 V063 17 16 15 14 13

Dear Reader,

As you continue your trip down *Scott Foresman Reading Street,* you will learn about yourself and others. You will improve your reading skills as you travel along!

What changes have you experienced as you have grown? What changes have you noticed in the world around you? The stories and articles in this book are all about changes.

Take time to enjoy yourself and the changes all around you as you continue along *Scott Foresman Reading Street!*

Sincerely,
The Authors

Changes

THE BIG ? **What is changing in our world?**

Unit 3 Contents

Week 6

Envision It! A Comprehension Handbook

Envision It! Visual Skills
Handbook EI•1–EI•9

Envision It! Visual Strategies
Handbook EI•11–EI•21

Don Leu
The Internet Guy

Right before our eyes, the nature of reading and learning is changing. The Internet and other technologies create new opportunities, new solutions, and new literacies. New reading comprehension skills are required online. They are increasingly important to our students and our society.

Those of us on the Reading Street team are here to help you on this new, and very exciting, journey.

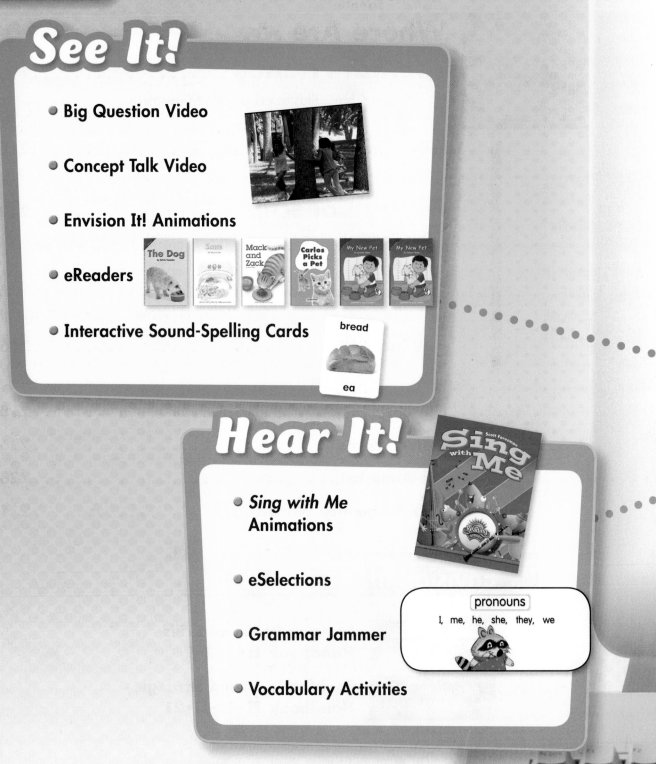

See It!

- Big Question Video

- Concept Talk Video

- Envision It! Animations

- eReaders

- Interactive Sound-Spelling Cards

bread

ea

Hear It!

- *Sing with Me Animations*

- eSelections

- Grammar Jammer

- Vocabulary Activities

pronouns
I, me, he, she, they, we

Concept Talk Video

| File | Edit | View | Favorites | Tools | Help |

http://www.ReadingStreet.com

Do It!

- Journal Word Bank

- Story Sort

- Letter Tile Drag and Drop   o s c m s

- Online Assessment

- Vocabulary Activities

THE BIG ?

**What is changing
in our world?**

Changes

Common Core State Standards

Speaking/Listening 1.a. Follow agreed-upon rules for discussions (e.g., listening to others with care, speaking one at a time about the topics and texts under discussion).

Oral Vocabulary

Let's Talk About

Read Together

Growing and Changing

- Share information about growing and changing.
- Share ideas about how places can change.

READING STREET ONLINE
CONCEPT TALK VIDEO
www.ReadingStreet.com

ENTERING
San Antonio
CITY LIMIT
POP. 1144646

Phonemic Awareness

Let's Listen for

Read Together

Sounds

- Find five things that contain the long e sound. Say the sound at the end of those words.

- Find two things that contain the long *i* sound. Say each sound in those words.

- Find two things that rhyme with *by*.

- Find something that rhymes with *funny*. Say each sound in that word.

READING STREET ONLINE
SOUND-SPELLING CARDS
www.ReadingStreet.com

Envision It! | Sounds to Know

bunny

-y

sky

-y

READING STREET ONLINE
SOUND-SPELLING CARDS
www.ReadingStreet.com

Phonics

Vowel Sounds of y

Words I Can Blend

b u d d y

f u z z y

f l y

r u s t y

wh y

Sentences I Can Read

1. His buddy shuts a rusty gate.

2. These fuzzy chicks can't fly.

3. Why did Jen run home?

Words I Can Read

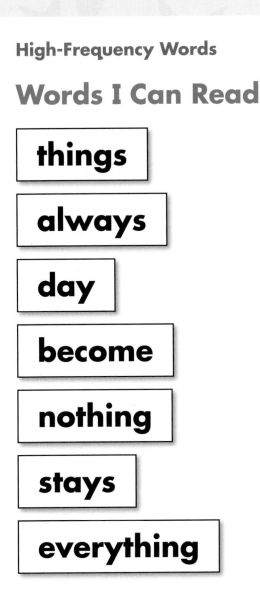

things

always

day

become

nothing

stays

everything

Sentences I Can Read

1. This frisky puppy will become a dog one day.

2. Everything in my desk always stays in its place.

3. Libby sees nothing in the sky but things that fly.

Common Core State Standards
Foundational Skills 3. Know and apply grade-level phonics and word analysis skills in decoding words.
Also Foundational Skills 2.b., 3.g.

Phonics

🎯 Syllable Pattern CV

Words I Can Blend

Sentences I Can Read

1. Kim said hi to me.

2. Dan will not be glad to go.

3. That game is so much fun!

I Can Read!

My pal Timmy and I always go to fun places. One day we met on Sandy Lane.

Timmy said, "Hi! Look! This used to be nothing but a muddy lot. Then men came to work. It has become a club for kids. We can do fun things, like skate, swim, and hike. Everything is free!"

"I am happy," I said. "I hope it stays!"

You've learned

- Vowel Sounds of y
- Syllable Pattern CV

High-Frequency Words

things always day nothing
stays become everything

A Place to Play

by Cynthia Chin-Lee

illustrated by Maryann Cocca-Leffler

Genre **Realistic fiction** tells about made-up events that could happen in real life. In this story you will read about a community that builds a new place to play.

Question of the Week

How do places change?

21

"This will be a fun day," Benny said to
Molly. "Nai Nai can take us to see where
Mom and Dad are working."

"I spy Dad and Mom!" said Benny.
"What are you doing?"

"We are planting things. This sunny spot
is good for growing plants," said Dad.

"It is muddy in that spot!" said Benny.

"Let us go inside," said Nai Nai.

"Here is a place for meetings," said Mom.
"Look, Benny! There is Ms. Torres!"

"Hi, Benny!" said Ms. Torres. "I grew up in
this neighborhood, so I want to help."

"This is a place for art," said Mom.
Look at the wall with **nothing** on it.
Now look at the wall next to it."

"That wall looks like my neighborhood!"
said Benny. "I see people working and
playing under a blue sky."

"Do you like it?" asked Mr. Gray.
Benny said, "Yes, I hope it stays
there always!"

"This will become a place to watch plays," said Dad.

"Look, there is Mr. Jackson," said Mom. "He lives by us too."

"People from the neighborhood came together to work on everything in this place," Mom said.

Benny saw a boy who seemed a little shy.
"Do you like to play ball?" Benny asked.

"Go check out this next one," said Dad.

"I will slide down!" Benny said.
Mom and Molly went up in the tower.

"They are lucky," said Nai Nai. "I wish I
had a place like this when I was a kid."

"See the sunset?" Mom asked.

Dad said, "It is time to go home."

"I like this place," said Benny.
"It is a good place for all of us!"

Common Core State Standards
Literature 1. Ask and answer questions about key details in a text.
Also Literature 2., Writing 5.

Envision It! | Retell

Think Critically

Read Together

1. Why might a community center be a good place to play? Text to World

2. Why do you think the author wrote this story? Author's Purpose

3. What do Benny and Molly see after they go inside? Sequence

4. Summarize the important ideas in the story. Summarize

5. Look Back and Write Look back at page 23. Why is a sunny spot good for growing plants? Write about it.

Key Ideas and Details • Text Evidence

Maryann Cocca-Leffler

Maryann Cocca-Leffler is an illustrator who also writes many of her own stories. She has gotten a lot of the inspiration for her stories from her two daughters. But she admits that she still thinks like a kid, and that helps when she writes children's books.

Here are other books by Maryann Cocca-Leffler.

Use the Reading Log in the *Reader's and Writer's Notebook* to record your independent reading.

Common Core State Standards
Writing 3. Write narratives in which they recount two or more appropriately sequenced events, include some details regarding what happened, use temporal words to signal event order, and provide some sense of closure. **Also Language 1.e.**

Let's Write It!

Read Together

Key Features of a Realistic Story

- characters and events seem real

- setting is like a real place

- story has a beginning, middle, and end

Narrative

Realistic Story

A **realistic story** is a made-up story that could happen in real life. The student model on the next page is an example of a realistic story.

Writing Prompt Think about a place to play that you think is interesting. Now write a made-up story about children playing at that place.

Writer's Checklist

Remember, you should . . .

☑ include characters, a setting, and events that seem real.

☑ include a beginning, middle, and end.

☑ use sentences and spell words correctly.

☑ use action verbs.

A Day at the Park

First, Dina finds a new park.
She brings Max the dog.
Then, Max wants to play.
Dina throws a ball to Max.
At last, Max wags his tail and runs. He brings the ball back to Dina.

**Genre
Realistic Story**
The setting could be a real place. The author wrote about a setting he or she found interesting.

**Writing Trait
Organization**
The story has a beginning, middle, and end.

These **action verbs** tell what characters do.

Conventions

- **Action Verbs**

- **Remember** An **action verb** tells what someone or something does.
   Max **runs**.

My Neighborhood, Then and Now

Read Together

Genre
Autobiography

- An autobiography is literary nonfiction. It is the true story of a person's life, written by that person.

- An autobiography includes events and feelings from that person's life.

- The author of an autobiography uses the word *I* to describe things that happened to him or her.

- Read "My Neighborhood, Then and Now." Look for elements that make this an autobiography.

My name is Emily. I am ten.

This is my neighborhood.

It has changed since I was little.

Tom's Toys

When I was four, my family planted a tree.

Let's **Think** About...

How do you know this is an autobiography? **Autobiography**

The tree is taller now.

Let's Think About...

Is this a true story or a fantasy? How do you know?
Autobiography

Our old library was small.

Now we have a big, new library.

I liked my neighborhood then.

I like my neighborhood now.

Let's Think About...

How did Emily feel about her neighborhood when she was little? How does she feel about it now?
Autobiography

Let's Think About...

Reading Across Texts Tell how Benny and Emily feel about their neighborhoods.

Writing Across Texts Make a list of what has changed in Benny's neighborhood and what has changed in Emily's neighborhood.

41

Common Core State Standards

Speaking/Listening 4. Describe people, places, things, and events with relevant details, expressing ideas and feelings clearly. **Also Foundational Skills 4.b., Language 5.**

I went on a long bike ride with my dad. It was fun! First, we rode to the park. Next, we rode to the lake ...

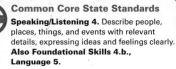

Let's **Learn** It!

Read Together

READING STREET ONLINE
VOCABULARY ACTIVITIES
www.ReadingStreet.com

Listening and Speaking

Get Ready For Grade 2

Use time-order transition words when you tell a story.

Tell About an Experience When we tell others about things that happen to us, we must speak clearly. We use words such as *first, next,* and *last* so our listeners can understand our story.

Practice It! Think of something that happened to you. Tell others about it. Use action verbs to tell what you did and use time-order transition words.

Vocabulary

An **antonym** is a word that means the opposite of another word.

wet

dry

Wet is an antonym of *dry*.

Practice It! Read these words.
Write and say antonyms for each one.

hot   huge   fast   sunny   go

Fluency

Accuracy and Rate Read the sentences. Be sure you read every word. Blend the sounds to read a new word. Ask yourself if it is a word you know. Check the new word in the sentence to see if it makes sense.

Practice It!

1. Kelly gave me a penny the other day.

2. My cat Misty likes to chase things.

3. It's always sunny when we go on trips.

Common Core State Standards

Speaking/Listening 4. Describe people, places, things, and events with relevant details, expressing ideas and feelings clearly.

Oral Vocabulary

Let's Talk About

Growing and Changing

- Share information about growing and changing.

- Share ideas about what we learn as we grow and change.

READING STREET ONLINE
CONCEPT TALK VIDEO
www.ReadingStreet.com

44

You've learned **150** **Amazing Words** so far this year!

45

Let's Listen for

Sounds

Read Together

- Find three things that rhyme with *think*. Say the sound at the end of those words.

- Find four things that are compound words.

- Find three things that rhyme with *wing*.

- Find a picture of a wing. Now add the sound /s/ in front of *wing*. Find a picture of the new word.

READING STREET ONLINE
SOUND-SPELLING CARDS
www.ReadingStreet.com

Common Core State Standards
Foundational Skills 3.b. Decode regularly spelled one-syllable words.
Also Foundational Skills 3.g.

Envision It! | Sounds to Know

swing

ng

skunk

nk

**READING STREET ONLINE
SOUND-SPELLING CARDS**
www.ReadingStreet.com

Phonics

Consonant Patterns *ng, nk*

Words I Can Blend

th i nk

b r i ng

th i ng

h o nk

s p r i ng

Sentences I Can Read

1. We think it will be late then.

2. She can bring me that red thing.

3. Will those geese honk this spring?

Words I Can Read

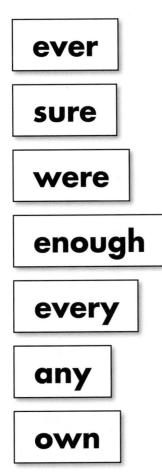

ever

sure

were

enough

every

any

own

Sentences I Can Read

1. She is not sure if that boy ever sang that song.

2. Were three boxes enough to fit every last bit of junk?

3. Hank can sip any of his own drinks.

Common Core State Standards
Foundational Skills 3.e. Decode two-syllable words following basic patterns by breaking the words into syllables.
Also Foundational Skills 3.g.

Envision It! | Sounds to Know

football

compound word

READING STREET ONLINE
SOUND-SPELLING CARDS
www.ReadingStreet.com

Phonics

Compound Words

Words I Can Blend

b a s e b a l l

s w i ng s e t

s a n d b o x

i n s i d e

l a p t o p

Sentences I Can Read

1. Tom and Tammy snack on nuts at baseball games.

2. The swingset is next to the sandbox.

3. Dad ran inside and got his laptop.

I Can Read!

Classmates Ling and Jess think baseball is the best thing ever invented. Last fall we were sure to see them every weekend. Those pals had enough skill to take on any kid! Games were fun.

Then this spring Ling fell off her bike and broke her hand. It is in a pink cast. Ling must sit in the stands until she is well. Jess must play on his own.

Ruby in Her Own Time

by Jonathan Emmett

illustrated by

Rebecca Harry

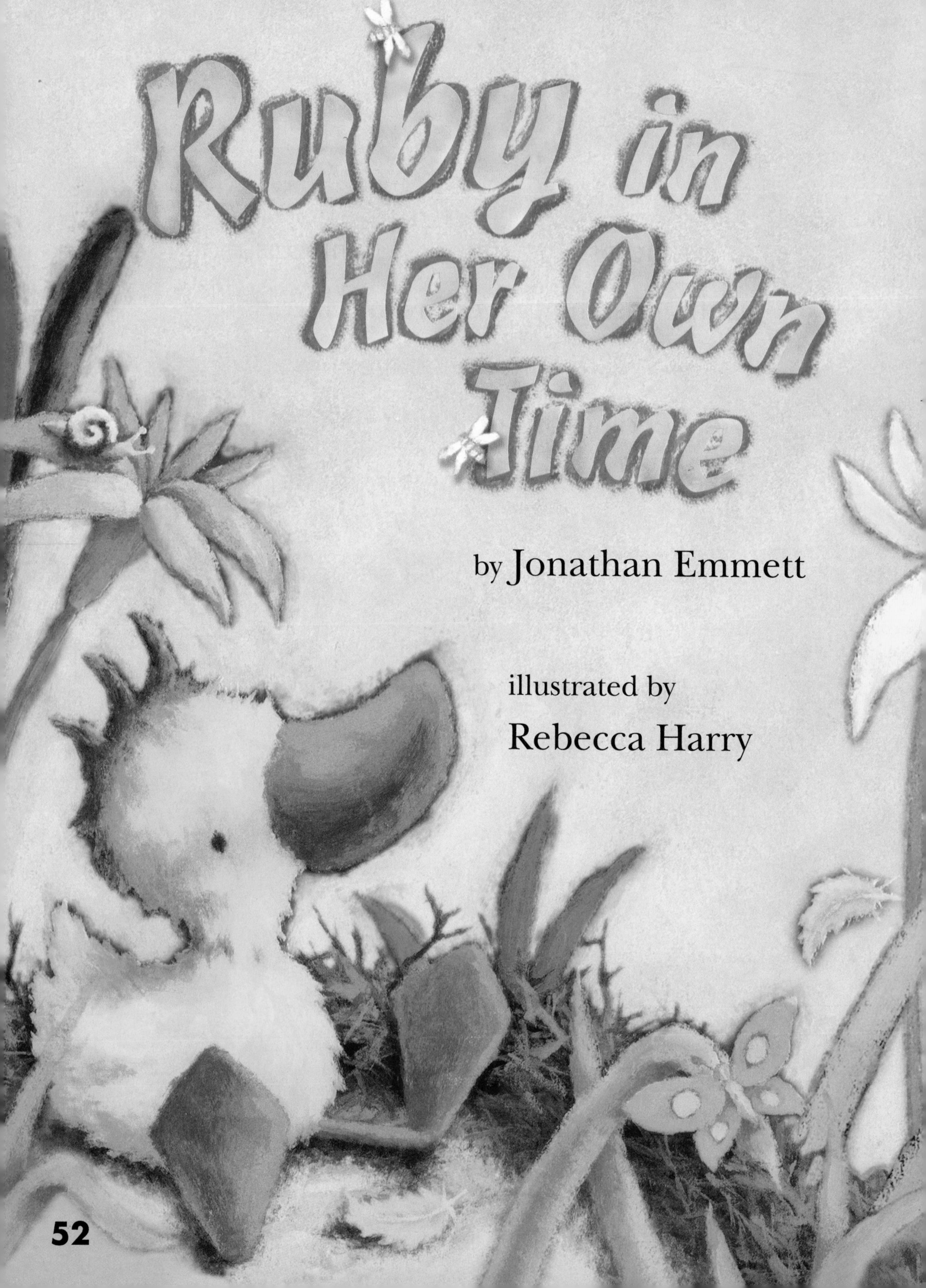

Read Together

Genre An **animal fantasy** is a story with animal characters that talk. Next you will read about a growing duck family.

Question of the Week

What do we learn as we grow and change?

Once upon a time upon a nest beside a lake, there lived two ducks—a mother duck and a father duck.

There were five eggs in the
nest. Mother Duck sat upon the
nest, all day and all night . . .

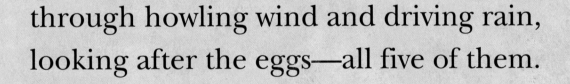

through howling wind and driving rain,
looking after the eggs—all five of them.

Then, one bright morning,
the eggs began to hatch.

One, two, three, four
little beaks poked out
into the sunlight.

One, two, three, four little ducklings shook their feathers in the breeze.

"We'll call them Rufus, Rory, Rosie, and Rebecca," said Father Duck. And Mother Duck agreed.

But the fifth egg did nothing.
"Will it ever hatch?" said Father Duck.

"It will," said Mother Duck, "in its own time."

And—
sure enough—
it did.

"She's very small," said Father Duck.
"What shall we call her?"

"We'll call her Ruby," said Mother Duck,
"because she's small and precious."

Rufus, Rory, Rosie, and Rebecca
ate whatever they were given.
They ate anything and everything.

But Ruby ate nothing.

"Will she ever eat?" said Father Duck.

"She will," said Mother Duck,
"in her own time."

And—
sure enough—
she did.

Rufus, Rory, Rosie, and
Rebecca swam off whenever
they were able.

They swam anywhere
and everywhere.

63

But Ruby swam nowhere.

"Will she ever swim?" said Father Duck.

"She will," said Mother Duck, "in her own time."

And—
sure enough—
she did.

Rufus, Rory, Rosie, and
Rebecca grew bigger.

And Ruby grew bigger too.
Her feathers grew out, and her
wings grew broad and beautiful.

And when Rufus, Rory, Rosie,
and Rebecca began to fly . . .

Ruby flew too!

Rufus, Rory, Rosie, and Rebecca flew far and wide. They flew out across the water. They flew up among the trees.

But Ruby flew farther
and wider. She flew out
beyond the water.

She flew up above
the trees.

She flew anywhere and everywhere.
She stretched out her beautiful wings
and soared high among the clouds.

Mother Duck and Father Duck watched Ruby flying off into the distance.

"Will she ever come back?" said Mother Duck.

"She will," said Father Duck, "in her own time."

And—
sure enough—
she did.

Common Core State Standards
Literature 1. Ask and answer questions about key details in a text.
Also Literature 9., Writing 5.

Think Critically

1. How have you changed from when you were a baby? Text to Self

2. What lesson does the author want you to learn? Author's Purpose

3. How is Ruby like the other ducks? How is she different?

   Compare and Contrast

4. Why do you think Ruby was the last duck to do everything? Inferring

5. **Look Back and Write**
   Look back at page 65. How does Ruby change as she gets bigger? Write about it.

   Key Ideas and Details • Text Evidence

Read Together

Jonathan Emmett

Jonathan Emmett got the idea for this story while jogging around a lake one morning. He saw a swan's nest, and the words *Once upon a time, upon a nest* popped into his head. He changed the swans to ducks, "and the story grew from there."

Mr. Emmett lives in England with his wife and two children.

Here are other books by Jonathan Emmett.

Bringing Down the Moon
Jonathan Emmett illustrated by Vanessa Cabban

Through the Heart of the Jungle
by Jonathan Emmett Illustrated by Elena Gomez

Reading Log

Use the Reading Log in the *Reader's and Writer's Notebook* to record your independent reading.

Common Core State Standards

Writing 1. Write opinion pieces in which they introduce the topic or name the book they are writing about, state an opinion, supply a reason for the opinion, and provide some sense of closure. **Also Literature 7., Language 1.c.**

Let's Write It!

Read Together

Key Features of Comments About a Story

- respond to the story
- tell what the writer thinks or feels

READING STREET ONLINE
GRAMMAR JAMMER
www.ReadingStreet.com

Comments About a Story

Comments about a story tell what you think of the story or part of the story. The student model on the next page is an example of comments about a story.

Writing Prompt Look at the pictures in *Ruby in Her Own Time*. Think about what Ruby does. Write sentences that tell two things Ruby does that you like.

Writer's Checklist

Remember, you should . . .

☑ tell about two parts of the story that you like.

☑ tell why you like them.

☑ use verbs in sentences, and spell words correctly.

I Like Ruby

I like when Ruby swims. It made me glad.

I like when Ruby comes back to her family. She has her own babies.

Conventions

• Verbs That Add -s

Remember A **verb** can tell what one person, animal, or thing does. Add **-s** to the verb. Say the verbs:

Ruby **swims**. A girl **runs**.

Common Core State Standards
Literature 1. Ask and answer questions about key details in a text.
Also Literature 9.

Genre
Fairy Tale

Read Together

- A fairy tale is a story with made-up characters that are sometimes animals.

- A fairy tale often begins with the phrase "Once upon a time." This phrase means that the story happened long ago, and that it is probably a fantasy.

- A fairy tale often ends with the phrase "They lived happily ever after." This phrase means that no matter what problems the characters have during the story, things get better for them later.

- As you read "The Ugly Duckling," look for elements of a fairy tale.

The Ugly Duckling

Once upon a time, Mother Duck's seven eggs hatched. Six of the ducklings looked alike. One was different.

Let's **Think** About...

This story begins with the phrase "Once upon a time." What does that tell you?
Fairy Tale

79

Let's **Think** About:...

How do you know this story is a fairy tale? **Fairy Tale**

The six ducklings thought the one was an ugly duckling.

The "ugly duckling" grew up to be a beautiful swan. The swan lived happily ever after.

Let's **Think** About...

What does it mean that the swan lived "happily ever after"? **Fairy Tale**

Let's **Think** About...

Reading Across Texts *Ruby in Her Own Time* and "The Ugly Duckling" are about animals that have problems. What problem does each animal have?

Writing Across Texts What do you think would happen if the swan in "The Ugly Duckling" were in Ruby's family? Write about it.

81

Common Core State Standards
Speaking/Listening 1.a. Follow agreed-upon rules for discussions (e.g., listening to others with care, speaking one at a time about the topics and texts under discussion). **Also Foundational Skills 4.b., Language 5.**

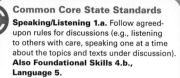

Let's Learn It!

Read Together

**READING STREET ONLINE
VOCABULARY ACTIVITIES**
www.ReadingStreet.com

Listening and Speaking

Get Ready For Grade 2

Be polite to your listeners.

Share Information and Ideas When we share ideas, we give everyone a turn to speak. When we listen, we pay attention to each speaker's ideas and opinions.

Practice It! Think about your favorite book. Tell others how you feel about it. Speak in complete sentences, using verbs that tell about now and correct subject-verb agreement. Be polite to your listeners.

Vocabulary

A **synonym** is a word that means the same as another word.

The ladybug is *little*.

The ladybug is *small*.

Little and *small* are synonyms.

Practice It! Read these words. Write and say a synonym for each one.

fast   **cute**   **cold**   **good**

Fluency

Appropriate Phrasing When you read, notice the punctuation marks. If a sentence ends with a question mark, your voice should go up at the end.

Practice It!

1. Did you bring enough for everyone?

2. Does she think we were going outside?

Common Core State Standards

Language 5.c. Identify real-life connections between words and their use (e.g., note places at home that are *cozy*).

Let's Talk About

Read Together

Growing and Changing

- Discuss animal life cycles.

- Discuss what we can learn about animals as they grow and change.

READING STREET ONLINE
CONCEPT TALK VIDEO
www.ReadingStreet.com

Let's Listen for

Sounds

Read Together

- Find three things that rhyme with *more*. Say the sound at the end of those words.

- Find the door. Say each sound in the word *door*.

- Find a picture of a shore. Now add the sound /t/ to the end of *shore*. Say the new word.

**READING STREET ONLINE
SOUND-SPELLING CARDS**
www.ReadingStreet.com

Common Core State Standards
Foundational Skills 3. Know and apply grade-level phonics and word analysis skills in decoding words.
Also Foundational Skills 2.d., 3.f., 3.g.

Envision It! | Sounds to Know

orchestra

or

score

ore

READING STREET ONLINE
SOUND-SPELLING CARDS
www.ReadingStreet.com

Phonics

r-Controlled *or, ore*

Words I Can Blend

p o r ch

sh o r t

c o r n

s t o r e

m o r e

Sentences I Can Read

1. We sat on the porch for a short time.

2. Can we get corn at that store?

3. Let's sing more songs.

Flor and Jim are best friends at school. Jim must go away for three weeks. He brushes his teeth, packs his bag, and gets in the car.

Flor rushes to his house. "This will be very sad, Jim," said Flor. "Our school will not be the same."

"Come back in three weeks, Flor," said Jim. "We can meet on my porch."

You've learned

- Ending -es; Plural -es
- Vowels: r-Controlled or, ore

High-Frequency Words

very   car   away   our
house   school   friends

91

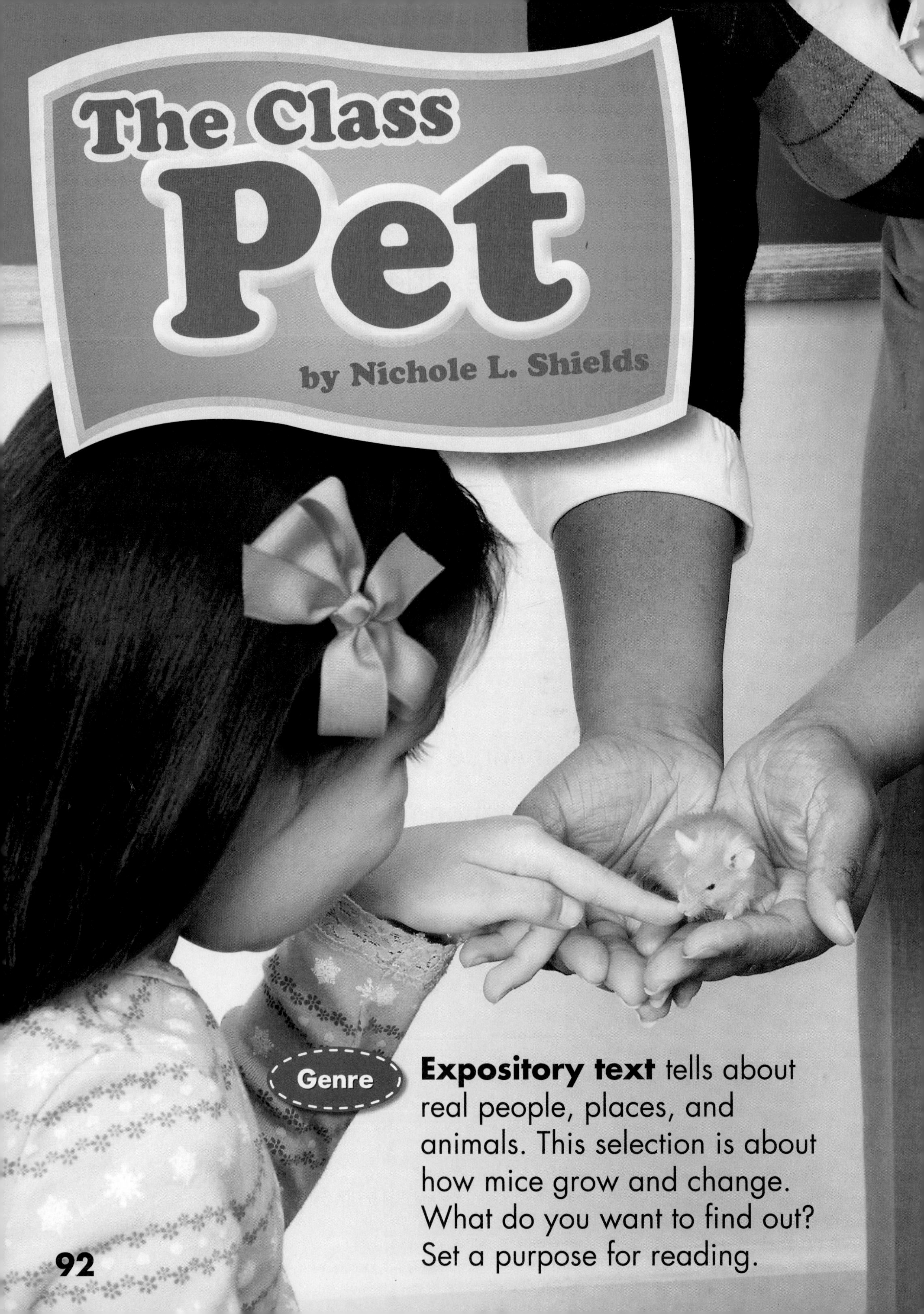

The Class Pet

by Nichole L. Shields

Genre

Expository text tells about real people, places, and animals. This selection is about how mice grow and change. What do you want to find out? Set a purpose for reading.

Question of the Week

What can we learn about animals as they grow and change?

Miss Ford takes a glass box to school.

"This will be a house for our class pet," Miss Ford tells the class.

The pet is a cute tan mouse.
The class names it Dory.

Miss Ford teaches lessons on pets.
She uses Dory in these lessons.

Dory is tan.

But mice can be black,
white, or brown.

Mice can have stripes
or spots too.

Mice need to eat and drink. Pet stores may sell seed mixes or hard pellets.

But mice will eat all sorts of things, such as corn and nuts.

Mice like to run and jump
late at night. It is time for them
to sleep when the sun rises.

Mice use torn cloth and cotton to make nests. Mice that live outside use grass and branches.

A mom can have lots of very small mice. Ten of them can be born at the same time. They nap in a nest.

When mice are born, they have no fur. These mice cannot see yet.

For a short time, small mice cannot eat seeds. They just sleep and drink milk. Time passes and small mice get fur.

More time passes and small mice can see. They can be away from the nest.

These mice can eat seeds and nuts like their mom.

Miss Ford tells the class that mice like friends. She tells the class that Dory wishes for one.

The next week, Miss Ford takes
a box from her car. In it is a mouse.
The class names it Cory. Dory and
Cory become friends.

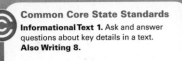
Envision It! Retell

Think Critically

Read Together

1. Why is a mouse a good pet to have in a classroom?

   Text to World

2. Why do you think the author wanted to write about mice? Author's Purpose

3. What is one fact about what mice eat? Fact and Opinion

4. How do the pictures help you understand how baby mice change as they grow? What can you do if you still don't understand?

   Monitor and Clarify

5. **Look Back and Write** Look back at page 100. Why do you think the mother mouse keeps the baby mice in the nest? Write about it.

   Key Ideas and Details • Text Evidence

Nichole L. Shields

Nichole L. Shields, an award-winning poet, never had a mouse as a class pet. In fact, her favorite mice are the cartoon characters she watched on television as a child!

Ms. Shields thinks it is important to learn about animals, and she wrote about mice to help teach children about how one kind of animal grows and changes.

Here are other books about how animals grow and change.

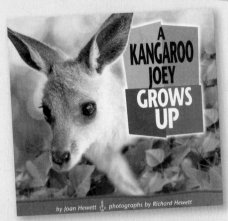

Use the Reading Log in the *Reader's and Writer's Notebook* to record your independent reading.

Let's Write It!

Read Together

Key Features of a Summary

- is about something you have read
- tells the most important information
- is short

READING STREET ONLINE
GRAMMAR JAMMER
www.ReadingStreet.com

Expository

Summary

A **summary** tells the most important ideas or events in a reading selection. The student model on the next page is an example of a summary.

Writing Prompt Write a summary of *The Class Pet*. Tell the most important events and ideas.

Writer's Checklist

Remember, you should . . .

☑ write sentences about **The Class Pet.**

☑ tell the most important ideas. Say your sentences.

☑ say and use the right verbs with singular and plural sentence subjects.

The Class Pet

The class gets a pet mouse. The children learn a lot about mice. Mice eat many things. They run around at night. They make nests. Baby mice need their mom. The class gets another mouse.

Writing Trait Conventions
The verbs go with the subjects. Say the sentences aloud.

Genre Summary
The writer tells important ideas from *The Class Pet*.

These **verbs** do not end in **-s**. They tell what children or mice do. Hear how the sentences sound.

Conventions

- ## Verbs with No Added -s

  Remember Do not add **-s** to a verb that tells what two or more people, animals, or things do.
  Jan and Mom **pack** boxes.

109

Common Core State Standards
Literature 1. Ask and answer questions about key details in a text.
Also Literature 5., 9.

Science in Reading

Genre
Fable

Read Together

- A fable is a short story.

- A fable has made-up characters that are often animals.

- The characters in a fable try to solve a problem.

- A fable often teaches a moral, or lesson. The reader can usually connect the meaning of the fable to his or her own experiences.

- As you read "Belling the Cat," look for elements of a fable.

- If you come to a part you don't understand, remember to reread that part aloud to help you make sense of what you're reading.

Belling the Cat

**a fable adapted from Aesop
illustrated by Viviana Garofoli**

The mice had a problem. There was a new cat in the house. It slept by the kitchen table. It hid behind doors. It raced down the hall toward the mice.

They could see its eyes in the dark. They could hear it howl at night. They never felt safe!

Let's Think About...

What might make you think so far that this story is a fable? **Fable**

Let's **Think** About...

What is the first step the mice take to solve their problem? **Fable**

The mice called a meeting. They had many ideas.

One little mouse pulled on his ear and said, "We need to hear that cat. Let's hang a bell on its neck."

Let's **Think** About...

How is this fable like an animal fantasy? **Fable**

113

Let's **Think** About...

What lesson do you think the mice will learn? **Fable**

All the mice went along with the idea. They cheered and clapped. They danced and laughed.

Then a wise old mouse asked,
"Who is going to bell the cat?"

Moral: Some things are easier said than done.

Let's **Think** About...

Can you connect the moral of this fable to your own experiences? How? **Fable**

Let's **Think** About...

Reading Across Texts How is Dory in *The Class Pet* different from the mice in "Belling the Cat"?

Writing Across Texts Think about Dory in *The Class Pet*. If she could talk, what would she say to the mice in "Belling the Cat"? Write the dialogue.

Let's Learn It!

Read Together

READING STREET ONLINE VOCABULARY ACTIVITIES
www.ReadingStreet.com

Listening and Speaking

Get Ready For Grade 2

Use your senses when you describe something.

Give Descriptions Good speakers use their senses when they describe something. They use words that tell how something looks, feels, sounds, and smells.

Practice It! Think of your favorite toy. Tell others about it. Use words to describe what it looks like, what it feels like, and how you use it. Speak in complete sentences, using correct subject-verb agreement.

116

Vocabulary

Descriptive words, or adjectives, tell how something is or feels.

happy   **sad**

Happy and *sad* describe how this girl feels.

Practice It! Read these descriptive words. Which words describe how you might feel if your team won a soccer game?

glad   **upset**   **afraid**   **excited**

Fluency

Appropriate Phrasing When you read, use the punctuation marks to show you how to read each sentence.

Practice It!

1. The school has more buses this year.

2. That storm had very strong winds!

3. Can we have corn with dinner?

Common Core State Standards

Speaking/Listening 1. Participate in collaborative conversations with diverse partners about grade 1 topics and texts with peers and adults in small and larger groups.

Let's Talk About

Read Together

Changes in Nature

- With a partner or in a group, discuss what is happening in the photographs on these pages. Listen to others to understand things in the photographs that you already know and things that you don't know anything about.

- Discuss plants and how they grow.

- Share ideas about changes that happen in a garden.

READING STREET ONLINE
CONCEPT TALK VIDEO
www.ReadingStreet.com

118

You've learned
1 6 7
Amazing Words
so far this year!

Common Core State Standards
Foundational Skills 2.c. Isolate and pronounce initial, medial vowel, and final sounds (phonemes) in spoken single-syllable words.

Let's Listen for

Sounds

Read Together

- Find the picture of a man's arm. Add the sound /h/ to the beginning of *arm*. Say the new word.

- Find something that rhymes with *yarn*. Say the sound in the middle of the word.

- Find something that rhymes with *charm*. Say the sound at the end of the word.

READING STREET ONLINE
SOUND-SPELLING CARDS
www.ReadingStreet.com

Common Core State Standards
Foundational Skills 3.f. Read words with inflectional endings.
Also Foundational Skills 3.g.

Envision It! | Sounds to Know

swimming

ending -ing

flipped

ending -ed

Phonics

Adding Endings

Words I Can Blend

s t o p p e d

p l a n n i ng

h o p p e d

d r i p p i ng

sh u t t i ng

Sentences I Can Read

1. Dad stopped planning his trip.

2. My rabbit hopped by the dripping hose.

3. Why is he shutting that box?

Words I Can Read

few

afraid

read

soon

how

again

Sentences I Can Read

1. A few kids stopped being afraid when we read that story.

2. We begged him to read us that funny joke again soon.

3. How many pages are we skipping?

Common Core State Standards
Foundational Skills 3. Know and apply grade-level phonics and word analysis skills in decoding words.
Also Foundational Skills 3.f., 3.g.

Envision It! | Sounds to Know

artist

ar

**READING STREET ONLINE
SOUND-SPELLING CARDS**
www.ReadingStreet.com

Phonics

🔊 Vowels: r-Controlled *ar*

Words I Can Blend

d a r k

s t a r t s

M a r ch

p a r k

t a r

Sentences I Can Read

1. Will it be dark when we get home?

2. Spring starts in March.

3. The lot by the park is patched with tar.

I Can Read!

Mark is good at getting things started. A few of us read how to start yard sales. It seemed like fun. But we were afraid that fitting in time for that is hard.

Soon Mark stopped by and got us going. Kids shopped at that sale again and again. It had games and stuff to read.

You've learned

- Adding Endings
- Vowels: *r*-Controlled *ar*

High-Frequency Words

few afraid read

soon how again

Frog and Toad Together

by Arnold Lobel

The Garden

 **Genre** In an **animal fantasy,** animals say and do things that people might say and do. Next you will read about two friends, Frog and Toad, who act a lot like people.

 Question of the Week

What changes happen in a garden?

Frog was in his garden.
Toad came walking by.

"What a fine garden you have, Frog,"
he said.

"Yes," said Frog. "It is very nice,
but it was hard work."

"I wish I had a garden," said Toad.

"Here are some flower seeds.
Plant them in the ground," said Frog,
"and soon you will have a garden."

"How soon?" asked Toad.

"Quite soon," said Frog.

Toad ran home.
He planted the flower seeds.

"Now seeds," said Toad, "start growing."

Toad walked up and down a few times. The seeds did not start to grow.

Toad put his head close to the ground and said loudly,

"Now seeds, start growing!"

Toad looked at the ground again. The seeds did not start to grow.

Toad put his head very close to the ground and shouted,

"NOW SEEDS, START GROWING!"

Frog came running up the path.
"What is all this noise?" he asked.

"My seeds will not grow," said Toad.

"You are shouting too much," said Frog.
"These poor seeds are afraid to grow."

"My seeds are afraid to grow?"
asked Toad.

"Of course," said Frog.
"Leave them alone for a few days.
Let the sun shine on them,
let the rain fall on them.
Soon your seeds will start to grow."

That night Toad looked out of his window.

"Drat!" said Toad. "My seeds have not started to grow. They must be afraid of the dark." Toad went out to his garden with some candles.

"I will read the seeds a story,"
said Toad. "Then they will not be afraid."

Toad read a long story to his seeds.

All the next day Toad
sang songs to his seeds.

And all the next day Toad
read poems to his seeds.

And all the next day Toad
played music for his seeds.

137

Toad looked at the ground.
The seeds still did not start to grow.

"What shall I do?" cried Toad.
"These must be the most frightened
seeds in the whole world!"

Then Toad felt very tired, and he fell asleep.

"Toad, Toad, wake up," said Frog. "Look at your garden!"

Toad looked at his garden.

Little green plants were coming up
out of the ground.

"At last," shouted Toad, "my seeds
have stopped being afraid to grow!"

"And now you will have a nice garden too," said Frog.

"Yes," said Toad, "but you were right, Frog. It was very hard work."

Common Core State Standards
Literature 1. Ask and answer questions about key details in a text. Also Writing 5.

Envision It! | Retell

142

Think Critically

1. What do plants need to help them grow? **Text to World**

2. Why do you think the author made some words in big letters? **Think Like an Author**

3. Why do you think Arnold Lobel wrote this story?

   Author's Purpose

4. What picture came to your mind when you read about Toad playing music for his plants? How did that help you understand what you were reading? **Visualize**

5. **Look Back and Write** Look back at page 134. What advice does Frog give to Toad? Write about it.

   Key Ideas and Details • Text Evidence

Arnold Lobel

When Arnold Lobel first wrote about Frog and Toad, there were not many books for beginning readers that were fun to read. Mr. Lobel used easy words, and children love those good friends Frog and Toad!

As a boy, Mr. Lobel liked to draw silly animal pictures for his friends. When he grew up, he wrote and illustrated almost one hundred books!

Here are other books by Arnold Lobel.

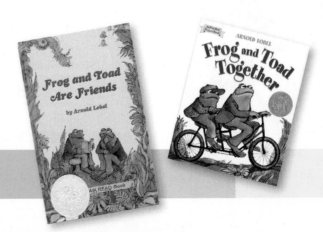

Use the Reading Log in the *Reader's and Writer's Notebook* to record your independent reading.

Common Core State Standards

Writing 2. Write informative/explanatory texts in which they name a topic, supply some facts about the topic, and provide some sense of closure. **Also Language 1.e.**

Let's Write It!

Read Together

Key Features of a List

- has words, phrases, or sentences written one below the other
- can include a heading

READING STREET ONLINE
GRAMMAR JAMMER
www.ReadingStreet.com

Lists

Lists are groups of words, phrases, or sentences. They are written one below the other. The student model on the next page is an example of lists.

Writing Prompt Think of actions Toad tried to help his garden grow. Write a list telling what Toad did that really helped the garden grow. In another list, tell his actions that did not help.

Writer's Checklist

Remember, you should . . .

☑ include a heading for each list.

☑ include parts from the story that fit on each list.

☑ write sentences with verbs.

Did Help

Toad planted seeds.
He will let the sun shine.

Did Not Help

Toad yelled at the seeds.
He played music.

Genre Lists
The sentences are one below the other.

Writing Trait Sentences The **sentences** tell about Toad.

These **verbs for past and for future** tell what Toad did before and will do soon.

Conventions

- **Verbs for Past and for Future**

- **Remember Verbs for the past** tell what someone or something did before. He **yelled**. **Verbs for the future** tell what someone or something will do or will be. She **will sing**.

145

Common Core State Standards

Informational Text 7. Use the illustrations and details in a text to describe its key ideas. **Also Informational Text 1.**

Genre

How-to Article

Growing Plants

- A how-to article tells us how to make or do something.

- Directions in how-to articles are made up of steps that are in the order in which they should be followed.

- Sometimes how-to articles have pictures that help us understand what we're supposed to do. The pictures can help us find specific information.

- Read "Growing Plants." As you read, think about what makes it a how-to article.

Do not be afraid to start a garden. It is not hard. Read how.

1. Plant a few seeds.

2. Let the sun shine on them.

3. Water the seeds again and again.

Soon you will be growing large plants.

1. seed

2. petal flower

stem

3. leaf

roots

Let's Think About...

What are the three steps to make a garden?
How-to Article

Let's Think About...

How do the pictures help you find specific information?
How-to Article

Let's Think About...

Reading Across Texts Compare the things Toad did to make a garden in *Frog and Toad Together* with the steps in "Growing Plants."

Writing Across Texts Write the steps Toad used to start a garden.

Common Core State Standards
Foundational Skills 4.b. Read on-level text orally with accuracy, appropriate rate, and expression on successive readings.

Let's
Learn
It!

Read Together

READING STREET ONLINE
VOCABULARY ACTIVITIES
www.ReadingStreet.com

Listening and Speaking

Get Ready For Grade 2

Add expression to your voice when you recite a poem.

Poetry Presentation When we read poetry aloud, we pay attention to the pattern of the words in the poem. We add expression to our voice so our listeners can enjoy the poem.

Practice It! Find a poem you like. Read it aloud to a partner. Use verbs to tell how you will read it to the class. Then read the poem to the class.

Vocabulary

A **dictionary** and a **glossary** show what a word means and how to spell it. The words are in alphabetical order.

Practice It! Put these words in alphabetical order. Then find them in the glossary or a dictionary.

sunset   **tower**   **mother**

Fluency

Expression and Intonation When you read something in quotation marks, read the way the character would say it.

Practice It!

1. "I tripped over the toy car!" yelled Peg.

2. "The race starts soon," Jack says.

3. "I hope to see you again," said Bart.

Common Core State Standards

Speaking/Listening 1. Participate in collaborative conversations with diverse partners about grade 1 topics and texts with peers and adults in small and larger groups.

Let's Talk About

Read Together

Changes in Nature

- Share ideas about what changes can be seen in nature.

- Discuss animal life cycles.

READING STREET ONLINE
CONCEPT TALK VIDEO
www.ReadingStreet.com

Common Core State Standards

Foundational Skills 2.c. Isolate and pronounce initial, medial vowel, and final sounds (phonemes) in spoken single-syllable words. **Also Foundational Skills 2.d.**

Phonemic Awareness

Let's Listen for

Sounds

- Find five pictures that contain the vowel sound in *turn*. Say all the sounds in one of the words.

- Find something that rhymes with *twirl*. Add the sound /z/ to the end of that word. Say the new word.

- Find something that rhymes with *shirt*. Say the sound in the middle. Now say the sound at the end.

READING STREET ONLINE
SOUND-SPELLING CARDS
www.ReadingStreet.com

Read Together

152

Common Core State Standards
Foundational Skills 3. Know and apply grade-level phonics and word analysis skills in decoding words.
Also Foundational Skills 3.g.

Envision It! | Sounds to Know

fern

er

girl

ir

curtains

ur

READING STREET ONLINE
SOUND-SPELLING CARDS
www.ReadingStreet.com

Phonics

r-Controlled
er, ir, ur

Words I Can Blend

h	e	r

g	i	r	l

sh	i	r	t

g	e	r	m	s

h	u	r	t

Sentences I Can Read

1. Her name is Jenny.

2. That girl wore a pink shirt.

3. Can germs hurt us?

Words I Can Read

know

push

done

wait

visit

Sentences I Can Read

1. We know Shirl likes it when we push her on that swing.

2. Stir this pot until that broth is done.

3. The nurse will wait while we visit Kurt.

Envision It! | Sounds to Know

you + are = you're

contraction

he + is = he's

contraction

we + have = we've

contraction

Phonics

Contractions

Words I Can Blend

w e ' r e

s h e ' s

w e ' v e

w h o ' s

i t ' s

Sentences I Can Read

1. We're glad she's back.

2. We've seen who's coming.

3. It's time for us to go.

Last week Peg sat in her yard after her work was done. She saw a tall girl by the brick home push her sister on a trike. Did she know all the kids on this block? Peg asked herself.

She didn't know that girl. They'd not met. Just then, a big van turned on her street. Men put stuff from that van in the brick home. Peg didn't wait. She said, "It's time to visit that girl."

You've learned

- Vowels: *r*-Controlled *er, ir, ur*
- Contractions

High-Frequency Words
know   push   done
wait   visit

Genre

Literary nonfiction is told like a story, but it's about something that really happens. Next you will read about the life cycle of a caterpillar.

I'm a Caterpillar

by Jean Marzollo
illustrated by Judith Moffatt

Question of the Week

What changes can be seen in nature?

I'm a caterpillar. **Munch. Crunch.**
I'm getting bigger! **Munch. Crunch.**

Munch. Crunch. Munch. Crunch.
That's it. No more food. I'm done.

It's time to hang from a stem.

I wait,

and wait,

and wait.

I shiver.
I twist.
I split my skin!

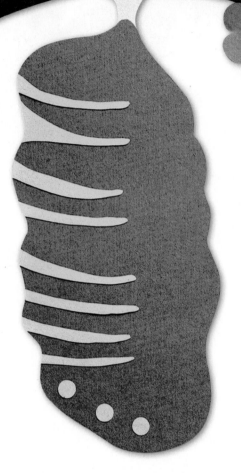

My old skin falls away.
I am soft inside.
I am a pupa.

I grow a shell
to protect the pupa.
I am now a chrysalis.

I keep changing.
Soon I'll come out.
What will I be?

A butterfly!

Push. Crack. Wow! I'm free!

My wings are all wet.

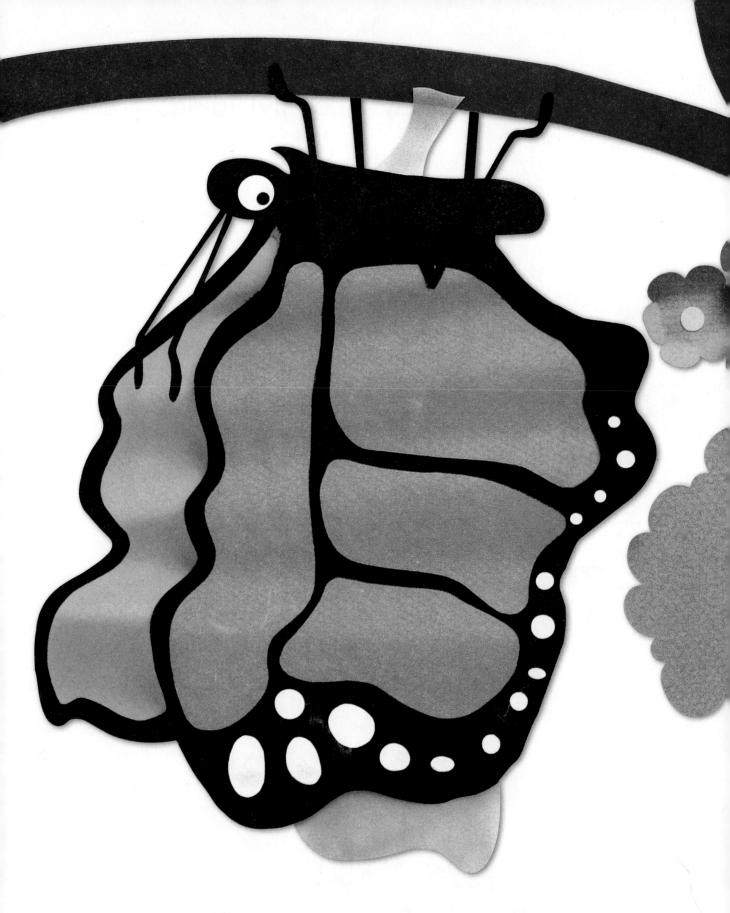

My wings dry off. They unfold.

Flap. Flap. Hey! I can fly! Ta-da!

I visit flowers. I drink nectar. Yum!

My mouth is like a straw.

Sip. Sip. Sip.

I have a mate. We visit many flowers.
We're not afraid of birds.
They know that we taste awful.

Soon I will lay my eggs.

The eggs have thin shells.

Baby caterpillars crawl out.

Hi! I'm a caterpillar.

Munch. Crunch.

What will happen to me next? Do you know?

caterpillar

chrysalis

eggs

butterfly

Common Core State Standards
Informational Text 1. Ask and answer
questions about key details in a text.
Also Writing 8.

Think Critically

1. What other animals have you read about that change? Text to Text

2. Why do you think the author ends the selection the same way it starts?

Think Like an Author

3. Name one fact you learned about caterpillars. Fact and Opinion

4. How does the order the author used to write this selection help you understand it better?

Text Structure

5. Look Back and Write
Why aren't the butterflies in this selection afraid of birds? Look back at page 170 and take notes. Then use your notes to write about why they aren't afraid of birds.

Key Ideas and Details • Text Evidence

Jean Marzollo

Jean Marzollo was a high school teacher and a magazine editor. Now she has written more than one hundred books for children! She writes about science, and she writes poetry, made-up stories, and *I Spy* books.

Ms. Marzollo likes to sew and work in her garden. She says writing is creative in the same way. It is hard and fun.

Here are other books by Jean Marzollo.

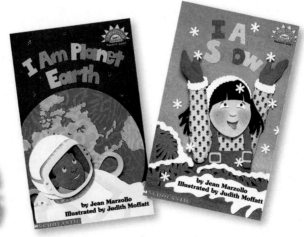

Use the Reading Log in the *Reader's and Writer's Notebook* to record your independent reading.

Common Core State Standards
Writing 2. Write informative/explanatory texts in which they name a topic, supply some facts about the topic, and provide some sense of closure. **Also Speaking/Listening 5., Language 1.e.**

Let's Write It!

Read Together

Key Features of Captions and Pictures

- captions tell about what the pictures show
- many captions are sentences

READING STREET ONLINE
GRAMMAR JAMMER
www.ReadingStreet.com

Descriptive

Captions and Pictures

A **caption** tells about a **picture**. The student model on the next page is an example of pictures and captions.

Writing Prompt Think of changes in nature. Plants and animals grow. Seasons change. Draw two pictures to show one way a plant or animal changes. Write captions about your pictures.

Writer's Checklist

Remember, you should . . .

☑ draw two pictures.

☑ tell about the pictures.

☑ focus on the idea of change.

☑ write complete sentences and say them aloud.

The leaves were green.

They are new colors.
It is fall.

Conventions

- **Verbs am, is, are, was, were**

  Remember The words **am, is,** and **are** tell about now.

- The words **was** and **were** tell about the past.

177

Common Core State Standards

Informational Text 5. Know and use various text features (e.g., headings, tables of contents, glossaries, electronic menus, icons) to locate key facts or information in a text.

21st Century Skills
INTERNET GUY

Computers are made up of many parts. The more you get to know each part, the easier it will be for you to use the computer.

Read Together

My Computer

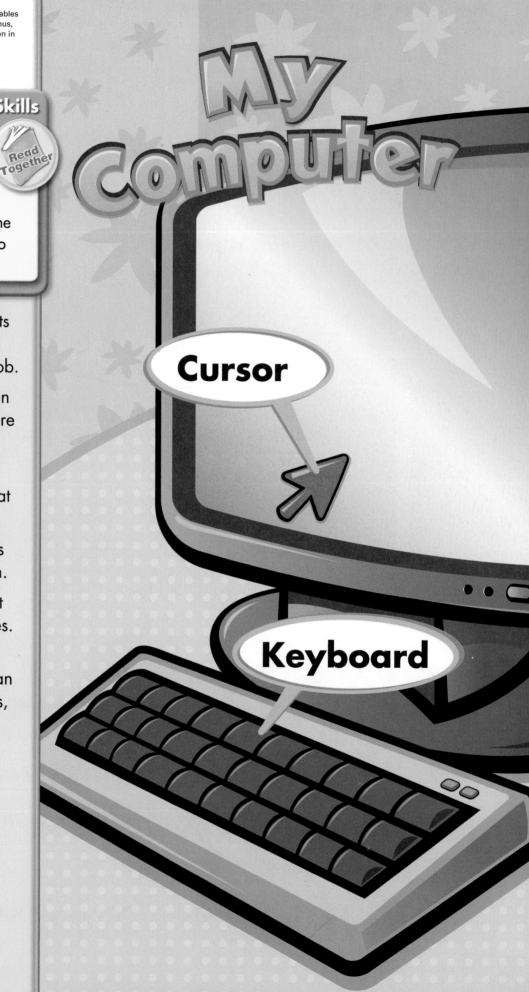

Cursor

Keyboard

- There are many parts to a computer. Each part has a special job.

- A cursor is usually an arrow. It shows where the next typed letter will appear.

- The keyboard is what we use to type.

- The monitor contains the screen we watch.

- The printer prints out documents or images.

- A CD-ROM is a compact disc that can contain text, pictures, movies, and sound.

- The mouse controls the cursor.

178

for more practice

Get Online!
www.ReadingStreet.com
Learn more about computers.

21st Century Skills Online Activity
Log on and follow the directions to learn more about the parts of a computer.

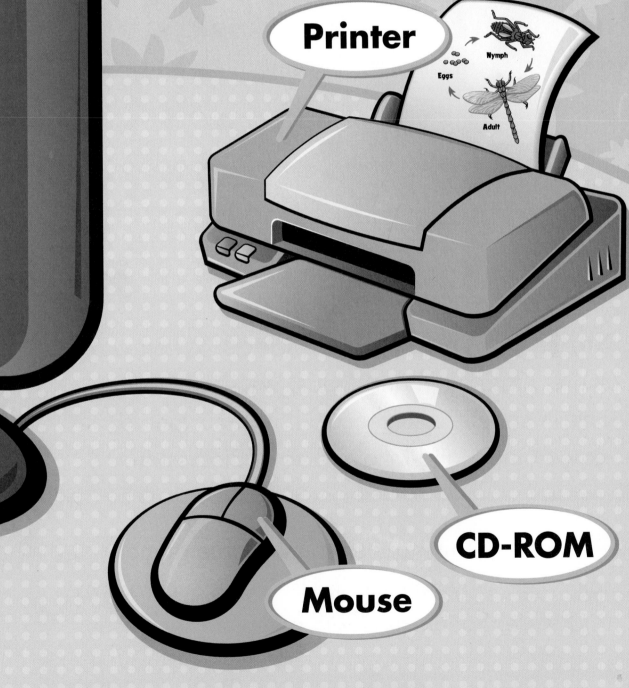

Monitor

Printer

Eggs
Nymph
Adult

CD-ROM

Mouse

Common Core State Standards
Speaking/Listening 1.a. Follow agreed-upon rules for discussions (e.g., listening to others with care, speaking one at a time about the topics and texts under discussion). **Also Foundational Skills 4.b.**

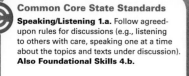

Let's **Learn** It!

Read Together

READING STREET ONLINE
VOCABULARY ACTIVITIES
www.ReadingStreet.com

My favorite game is tag because I like to run. One time, we played tag at ...

Get Ready For Grade 2

Follow agreed-upon rules for discussion.

Listening and Speaking

Share Information and Ideas When we share information and ideas, we speak clearly and in complete sentences. It is important to stay on topic and follow rules of discussion.

Practice It! Think about your favorite game. Tell others why you like it. Use verbs such as *was* and *were*. Speak clearly in complete sentences.

Vocabulary

A **glossary** lists some of the words found in a book.

boy   A **boy** is a male child.

shiver   To **shiver** is to shake.

Boy and *shiver* are in your glossary. They are listed in alphabetical order.

Practice It! Read these words. Put them in alphabetical order, and then find them in the glossary or a dictionary.

father   **warm**   **night**

Fluency

Expression and Intonation When you read, use your voice to make the sentences more interesting.

Practice It!

1. Are you going to visit your sister?

2. I know I want that shirt!

3. Let's wait for everyone to have one turn.

Let's Talk About

Read Together

Changes in Nature

- Contribute to a discussion about differences among the four seasons.

- Discuss animal behavior.

- Share information about what animals do when the seasons change.

READING STREET ONLINE
CONCEPT TALK VIDEO
www.ReadingStreet.com

Common Core State Standards

Foundational Skills 2.d. Segment spoken single-syllable words into their complete sequence of individual sounds (phonemes). **Also Foundational Skills 2.c.**

Let's Listen for

Read Together

Sounds

- Find five pictures that contain the sound /j/.

- Find something that rhymes with *ridge*. Say each sound in the word.

- Find something that rhymes with *ledge*. Say the last sound in the word.

- Find something that rhymes with *dodge*. Add the sound /s/ to the end. Say the new word.

READING STREET ONLINE
SOUND-SPELLING CARDS
www.ReadingStreet.com

MAYOR

184

Common Core State Standards
Foundational Skills 3.f. Read words with inflectional endings.
Also Foundational Skills 3., 3.g.

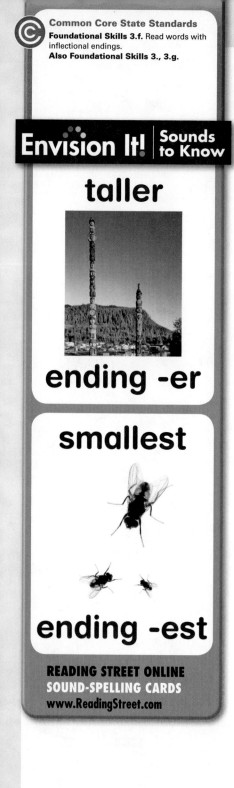

Envision It! | Sounds to Know

taller

ending -er

smallest

ending -est

Phonics

Comparative Endings -er, -est

Words I Can Blend

b i g g e s t

t a l l e s t

h o t t e r

f a s t e r

h a r d e s t

Sentences I Can Read

1. He ate the biggest plum from the tallest tree.

2. Is summer hotter than winter?

3. We think faster when we work at the hardest task.

Words I Can Read

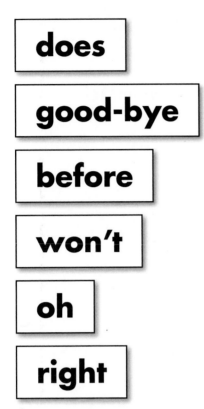

does

good-bye

before

won't

oh

right

Sentences I Can Read

1. Does the smallest girl wave good-bye before you go?

2. We won't be quicker than he is.

3. Oh, no! We're right next to the deepest hole.

© Common Core State Standards
Foundational Skills 2.b. Orally produce single-syllable words by blending sounds (phonemes), including consonant blends. **Also Foundational Skills 3., 3.f., 3.g.**

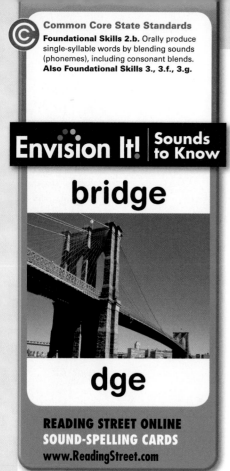

Envision It! | Sounds to Know

bridge

dge

READING STREET ONLINE
SOUND-SPELLING CARDS
www.ReadingStreet.com

Phonics

Consonant Pattern -*dge*

Words I Can Blend

b | a | dge

j | u | dge

e | dge

p | l | e | dge

b | r | i | dge

Sentences I Can Read

1. Which badge can we get?

2. That judge is sitting on the edge of her bench.

3. We made this pledge that we will cross that bridge.

Sally kisses her mom good-bye before lunch. She walks right next to the hedge and calls, "Fluffy, I am the saddest girl in the world. Won't you sit with me and purr?"

Does Fluffy run to Sally? Oh, no! Fluffy runs deeper into the hedge. Why does Fluffy run? Sally squeezes harder than Fluffy likes.

Later Sally makes a pledge to be nice to Fluffy. After that, Fluffy never runs from Sally!

You've learned

- Comparative Endings *-er, -est*
- Consonant Pattern *-dge*

High-Frequency Words
does good-bye before
won't oh right

189

Where Are My Animal Friends?

by William Chin
illustrated by Scott Gustafson

Genre A **drama,** or play, is a story that is written to be acted out. Next you can read and then act out a play about animal friends who get ready for winter.

Question of the Week

What do animals do when the seasons change?

Characters

Raccoon

Goose

Bear

Hummingbird

Squirrel

Hello, Goose! Why are you shivering?

 This forest is chilly, Raccoon.
The days are shorter now. And it's
getting colder every day.

 Then we don't have much time
to find our friends.

 You're right, Raccoon. Let's look
for Caterpillar.

Caterpillar lives in this tree.
But where are all the leaves?

 Many of them are on the ground.
Where is Caterpillar?

Look, here comes the smallest bird in the forest. Hello, Hummingbird! Have you seen Caterpillar?

Oh, yes. Caterpillar is right here.

 That's not Caterpillar! Caterpillar is long. This thing is not long.

 Our friend Caterpillar moves a lot. This thing does not move at all.

But Caterpillar is inside.

 Then we won't see Caterpillar until spring, when he'll be a butterfly.

Well, I'm glad you will be here for the winter.

 Oh, no, Raccoon. I can't stay. I must fly away to where it is warm. Hummingbird must too.

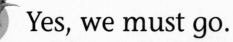 Yes, we must go.

Oh, my! I am the saddest raccoon in the forest. Will you come back?

 Yes, we'll be back in the spring. Good-bye, Raccoon!

 Good-bye, Goose! Good-bye, Hummingbird! I will see if Bear is at home.

Hello, Bear!

 Hello, Raccoon. Is it spring yet?

 No, not yet. It will be winter before it is spring. Why are you sleeping?

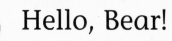 I ate and ate all summer. Now I am fatter than before, and I don't need to eat. I will sleep a long time. I won't budge until spring.

Oh, no! All my friends are going away!

 Pardon me, but I'm sleepy. Good night, Raccoon!

Good night, Bear. But who will be my friend? Oh, here comes Squirrel.

Hello, Raccoon. Where is everyone?

 Goose flew away, and so did Hummingbird. We won't see Caterpillar until spring, and Bear is sleeping for the winter. Are you going away too?

Oh, no. I will stay here all winter.
I have a warm nest and lots of food.
Will you play with me?

Yes, Squirrel! Let's race to the edge of the forest and back!

Put On a Play!

What you will need:

Costumes

Costumes can be simple or fancy.

Props

One prop you will
need for this play is
a chrysalis. Will you
need anything else?

Scenery

Simple sets can show that the play is set in a forest in the fall.

An Audience

Practice your parts. Then ask another class to come to the play!

Common Core State Standards
Literature 1. Ask and answer questions about key details in a text.
Also Literature 2., Writing 5.

Envision It! | Retell

Think Critically

Read Together

1. What do you remember about how a caterpillar changes? Text to Text

2. What does the author want you to learn from this play? Author's Purpose

3. Why are the animals in a hurry to find their friends?

   Draw Conclusions

4. How do you know which line to read in a play?

   Background Knowledge

5. **Look Back and Write** Look back at pages 198 and 199. Where do animals go when the days turn cold? Write about it.

   Key Ideas and Details • Text Evidence

William Chin

William Chin likes the winter. He lives in Chicago, where it gets cold in winter. His daughter is a figure skater. He and his wife skate too.

Mr. Chin sang in musicals in school. Now he is a choir director. He works with a children's choir. He is also a conductor for the Chicago Symphony Chorus.

Here are more books about winter.

Use the Reading Log in the *Reader's and Writer's Notebook* to record your independent reading.

Common Core State Standards

Writing 3. Write narratives in which they recount two or more appropriately sequenced events, include some details regarding what happened, use temporal words to signal event order, and provide some sense of closure. **Also Language 1., 2.d.**

Let's Write It!

Read Together

Key Features of a Play Scene

- is written to be acted for an audience
- characters have lines to say

READING STREET ONLINE
GRAMMAR JAMMER
www.ReadingStreet.com

Play Scene

A **play scene** is part of a play. The student model on the next page is an example of a short play scene.

Writing Prompt Think about Raccoon and Squirrel in *Where Are My Animal Friends?* What would they say if they could call Goose on a phone? Write a play scene showing what they would say.

Writer's Checklist

Remember, you should . . .

☑ use each character's name to show who speaks.

☑ write words for the characters to say.

☑ write about Raccoon, Squirrel, and Goose.

Raccoon: Hello. We miss you, Goose.

Squirrel: How are you?

Goose: It is hot here.

Raccoon: When will you be back?

Goose: Spring is the time!

Squirrel: We can't wait!

Genre
Play Scene
The words show what the characters say.

Writing Trait
Sentences The characters talk to each other in **sentences**.

Can't is a **contraction** made from **can** and **not**. Say the contraction *can't*.

Conventions

- ## Contractions with Not

  Remember A **contraction**
- puts two words together. A contraction has an apostrophe. Say **hasn't**. (has + not)

211

Common Core State Standards
Literature 4. Identify words and phrases in stories or poems that suggest feelings or appeal to the senses. **Also Literature 10.**

This Tooth

Genre
Poetry

- Poems are written in lines and stanzas. Stanzas are groups of lines in a poem.

- Poems often have rhyme, or words with the same middle and ending sounds. They usually have rhythm, or a regular pattern of beats.

- Some poems have alliteration, or words close to each other with the same beginning sound.

- Read the poems. Look for elements of poetry as you read.

I jiggled it
    jaggled it
        jerked it.

I pushed
    and pulled
    and poked it.

But—
As soon as I stopped,
and left it alone,
This tooth came out
on its very own!

by Lee Bennett Hopkins
illustrated by David Diaz

Tommy

I put a seed into the ground
And said, "I'll watch it grow."
I watered it and cared for it
As well as I could know.

One day I walked in my
back yard,
and oh, what did I see!
My seed had popped
itself right out,
Without consulting me.

by Gwendolyn Brooks
illustrated by David Diaz

Let's Think About...

Find the **alliteration** in "This Tooth." Which words begin with the same sound?

Let's Think About...

Which lines **rhyme** in the first stanza of "Tommy"? Which lines rhyme in the second stanza?

Where Do Fish Go in Winter?

When lakes turn to ice
And are covered with snow,
What becomes of the fish
Who are living below?

It's not so exciting
Down under the ice,
But fish find it restful
And really quite nice.

It's dark and it's cold,
But the water's not frozen.
In fact, it's just perfect
For fish to repose in.

Let's **Think** About...

What are the **rhyming** words in this poem?

They breathe very little.
Their swimming gets slower.
Each fish makes his heart rate
Go lower and lower.

And except for occasional
Lake bottom treats,
The whole winter long
The fish hardly eats.

by Amy Goldman Koss
illustrated by Laura J. Bryant

Let's Think About...

What is the **rhythm** in this poem? As you read the poem, clap your hands to show the beats.

Let's Think About...

Reading Across Texts *Where Are My Animal Friends?*, "This Tooth," "Tommy," and "Where Do Fish Go in Winter?" each tell about a change. Describe each change.

Writing Across Texts Use rhythm and rhyme to write a short poem about fall and what happens then. Try to use words that begin with the same sound, such as *lovely leaves* or *falling fast*.

Common Core State Standards
Speaking/Listening 1.a. Follow agreed-upon rules for discussions (e.g., listening to others with care, speaking one at a time about the topics and texts under discussion). **Also Foundational Skills 4.b., Language 4., 4.a.**

On Thursday, we will be having art class. Don't forget your paint smock. We will be leaving at ...

Let's Learn It!

Read Together

READING STREET ONLINE
VOCABULARY ACTIVITIES
www.ReadingStreet.com

Listening and Speaking

Get Ready For Grade 2

Speak clearly and slowly when making an announcement.

Make an Announcement When we make an announcement, we make sure to speak clearly and slowly. Good announcements include all the important information.

Practice It! Look at your class's calendar. Announce to the class something that is coming up. Speak clearly and use complete sentences with correct subject-verb agreement.

Vocabulary

If a word has more than one meaning, **context clues** can help you figure out which meaning is being used. The word *ring* can mean "jewelry you wear on your finger." *Ring* can also mean "to make a sound like that of a bell."

Practice It! Read these sentences. What is the meaning of the word *ring* in each sentence?

I can hear the buzzer **ring.**

Cindy's mother gave her a sparkly **ring.**

Fluency

Expression and Intonation When you read, try to read as if you are talking. Use your voice to make the sentences interesting.

Practice It!

1. Look around when you reach the edge.

2. That judge thinks my sheep will win.

3. Oh, the ledge is taller over there!

art • butterfly

Aa

art Painting and drawing are ways to create **art.**

Bb

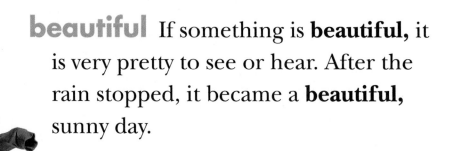
boy

beautiful If something is **beautiful,** it is very pretty to see or hear. After the rain stopped, it became a **beautiful,** sunny day.

boy A **boy** is a male child. A **boy** grows up to be a man.

brown **Brown** is a dark color like that of chocolate.

butterfly A **butterfly** is an insect with two pairs of large, usually brightly-colored wings.

Cc

caterpillar A **caterpillar** is an insect that looks like a furry worm. **Caterpillars** turn into moths or butterflies.

caterpillar

chrysalis A caterpillar becomes a **chrysalis** when it grows a hard shell around itself.

crawl When you **crawl,** you move on your hands and knees or with your body close to the ground. Worms, snakes, and lizards **crawl.**

Ff

father A **father** is a man who has a child or children.

feather A **feather** is one of the light, soft things that cover a bird's body.

feather

flew • grew

 flew The bird **flew** away. We **flew** to New York in an airplane.

fur **Fur** is the soft, thick hair that covers the skin of many animals.

Gg **goose** A **goose** is a large bird with a long neck. A **goose** looks like a duck but is larger.

goose

grew The grass **grew** very fast from all the rain.

ground The **ground** is the soil or dirt on the surface of the Earth. The **ground** was rocky.

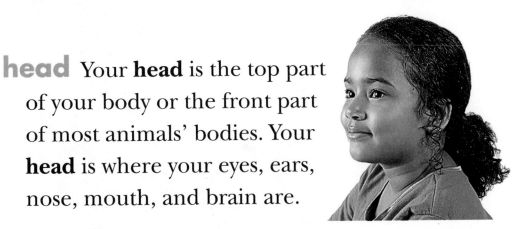

head

Hh

head Your **head** is the top part of your body or the front part of most animals' bodies. Your **head** is where your eyes, ears, nose, mouth, and brain are.

howling When something is **howling,** it is making a long, loud noise. The wind is **howling** tonight.

Mm

mother A **mother** is a woman who has a child or children.

mother

mouse A **mouse** is a small animal with soft fur and a long, thin tail.

night • precious

Nn

night **Night** is the time between evening and morning.

night

now **Now** means at this time. Please take the dog out **now.**

Pp

precious **Precious** means having great value. Mom's ring is very **precious** to her.

precious

pupa The **pupa** is the form of an insect while it is changing from a wormlike larva into an adult.

raccoon A **raccoon** is a small animal with thick fur. Its tail is long and has rings of a different color. **Raccoons** look for food at night.

raccoon

rain **Rain** is the water that falls in drops from the clouds. The **rain** made us all wet as we walked home from school.

rain

shiver • sunset

Ss

shiver To **shiver** is to shake.

shouted When you have **shouted,** you have called out or yelled loudly. He **shouted** for help.

shouted

shouting When you are **shouting,** you are calling or yelling.

spring **Spring** is the season of the year between winter and summer. **Spring** is the season when plants begin to grow.

sunset **Sunset** is the time when the sun is last seen in the evening.

sunset

Tt

teaches If a person **teaches** something, he or she helps someone learn. He **teaches** people how to play the piano.

tower

tower A **tower** is a tall building or part of a building. A **tower** may stand alone or may be part of a church, castle, or other building.

Ww

warm If something is **warm,** it is more hot than cold. The water is **warm** enough to swim in. He sat in the **warm** sunshine.

Yy

year A **year** is from January 1 to December 31. A **year** is 12 months long. There are four seasons in a **year:** winter, spring, summer, and fall.

225

A Place to Play

always
become
day
everything
nothing
stays
things

The Class Pet

away
car
friends
house
our
school
very

Ruby in Her Own Time

any
enough
ever
every
own
sure
were

Frog and Toad Together

afraid
again
few
how
read
soon

I'm a Caterpillar

done
know
push
visit
wait

Where Are My Animal Friends?

before
does
good-bye
oh
right
won't

Aa Bb Cc

Dd Ee Ff

Gg Hh Ii

Jj Kk Ll

Mm Nn Oo

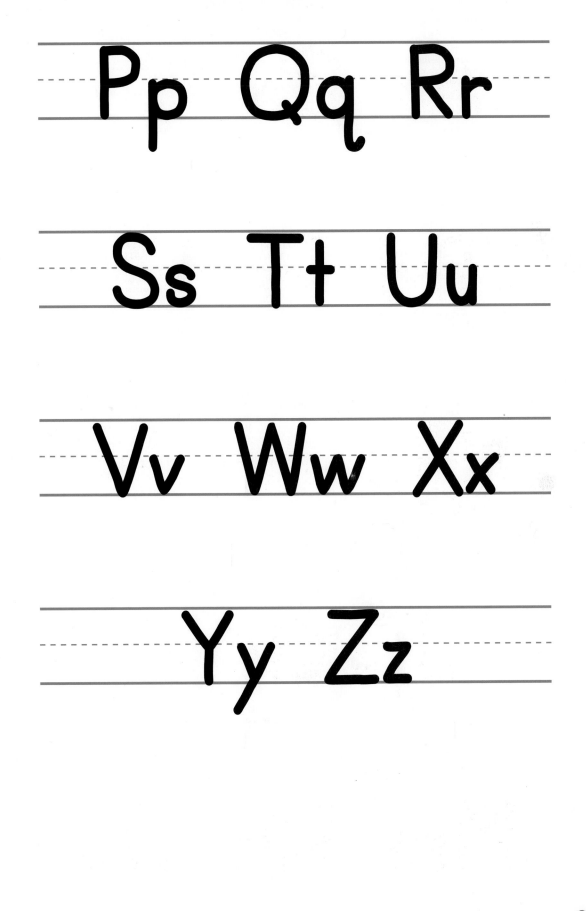

Pp Qq Rr

Ss Tt Uu

Vv Ww Xx

Yy Zz

Acknowledgments

Text

Grateful acknowledgment is made to the following for copyrighted material:

Brooks Permissions

"Tommy" by Gwendolyn Brooks from *Bronzeville Boys And Girls*. Copyright © 1956, renewed Copyright © 1984 Gwendolyn Brooks Blakely. Reprinted by consent of Brooks Permissions.

Cartwheel Books, a division of Scholastic, Inc.

From *I'm a Caterpillar* by Jean Marzollo, illustrated by Judith Moffat. A Hello Science Reader! Book published by Cartwheel Books/Scholastic Inc. Text copyright © 1997 by Jean Marzollo, illustrations copyright © 1997 by Judith Moffat.

Curtis Brown, Ltd.

"This Tooth" by Lee Bennett Hopkins. Copyright © 1970 by Lee Bennett Hopkins. First appeared in ME!, published by Seabury Press. Used by permission of Curtis Brown, Ltd.

Dial Books for Young Readers, a Member of Penguin Group (USA) Inc.

"Where Do Fish Go in Winter?" from *Where Fish Go in Winter and Other Great Mysteries* by Amy Goldman Koss and illustrated by Laura J. Bryant. Copyright © 1987 Amy Goldman Koss, text. Copyright © 2002 by Laura J. Bryant, illustrations. Used by permission of Dial Books for Young Readers, A Division of Penguin Young Readers Group, A Member of Penguin Group (USA) Inc., 345 Hudson Street, New York, NY 10014. All rights reserved.

HarperCollins Publishers

"The Garden" by Arnold Lobel from *FROG AND TOAD TOGETHER*. Text Copyright © 1971, 1972 by Arnold Lobel. Used by permission of HarperCollins Publishers.

Scholastic, Inc.

From *Ruby in Her Own Time* by Jonathan Emmett, illustrations by Rebecca Harry. Text copyright © 2003 by Jonathan Emmett, illustrations copyright © 2003 by Rebecca Harry. Used by permission of Scholastic, Inc.

Note: Every effort has been made to locate the copyright owner of material reproduced on this component. Omissions brought to our attention will be corrected in subsequent editions.

Cover: (B) ©Theo Allots/Getty Images, (T) Getty Images

Illustrations

EI2–EI9 Mary Anne Lloyd; **EI12–EI21** Chris Lensch; **14-15** NathanHale; **20-36** Maryann Cocca-Leffler; **38-41** Nan Brooks; **46-47** Steve Simpson; **78-81** Paul Eric Roca; **86-87** Dani Jones; **110-115** Viviana Garofoli; **120-121** Erwin Haya; **152-153** Orlando Ramirez; **184-185** Ron Lieser; **190-205** Scott Gustafson; **212, 213** David Diaz; **214-215** Laura J. Bryant

Photographs

Every effort has been made to secure permission and provide appropriate credit for photographic material. The publisher deeply regrets any omission and pledges to correct errors called to its attention in subsequent editions.

Unless otherwise acknowledged, all photographs are the property of Pearson Education, Inc.

Photo locators denoted as follows: Top (T), Center (C), Bottom (B), Left (L), Right (R), Background (Bkgd)

12 (Bkgd) ©Joseph Sohm/Visions of America/Corbis, (T) ©Rudy Sulgan/Corbis; **16** ©Morales Morales/PhotoLibrary Group, Ltd., Getty Images; **18** ©Benjamin Rondel/Corbis, ©David R. Frazier Photolibrary, Inc./Alamy Images, ©Pixland; **42** (T) Don Mason Photography; **43** (B) ©Larry Williams/Corbis, (C) ©Photomorgana/Corbis; **44** (TR) ©Jim Craigmyle/Corbis, (BL) ©Royalty-Free/Corbis, (BR) ©Tom & Dee Ann McCarthy/Corbis, (TL) Digital Vision; **45** (B) ©Rana Faure/Getty Images; **48** ©Tom Brakefield/Corbis; **50** Getty Images; **83** Radius Images/Jupiter Images; **84** (Bkgd) ©Lynn M. Stone/Nature Picture Library, (B) ©Rolf Nussbaumer/Nature Picture Library; **85** ©Rolf Nussbaumer/Nature Picture Library; **88** ©GoGo Images/Alamy, Getty Images; **90** ©Laura Ashley/Alamy, ©Miro Vintoniv/PhotoLibrary Group, Inc.; **96** (CL) ©De Meester/ARCO/Nature Picture Library, (BL) ©DK Images, (TL) Emilia Stasiak/iStockphoto; **97** (B) Stephen Hayward/©DK Images; **99** (B) Jane Burton/©DK Images; **100** (B) ©Jane Burton/Nature Picture Library; **101** (B) ©Jose B. Ruiz/Nature Picture Library, (C) Kim Taylor/©DK Images; **102** (B) ©Barrie Watts/©DK Images; **103** (B) ©Jane Burton/Nature Picture Library; **118** ©Max Spreewald/Getty Images; **119** (TL) ©Robert Harding Picture Library Ltd/Alamy Images, (BR) ©Roger Ball/Corbis; **122** ©David Turnley/Corbis, ©Ryan McVay/Getty Images; **124** ©Blend Images/Alamy; **146** (B) Dave King/DK Images; **147** (CL) ©D. Boone/Corbis, (BL) William Taufic/Corbis; **150** Getty Images; **151** ©Eric Baccega/Nature Picture Library, ©Ross Hoddinott/Nature Picture Library; **154** ©MIXA Co., Ltd./Alamy, ©Olivier Asselin/Alamy, ©Radius Images/Photolibrary; **182** (B) ©George McCarthy/Corbis; **183** (BR) ©Jacana/Photo Researchers, Inc., (C) ©Steve Kaufman/Corbis; **186** ©Ben Welsh/PhotoLibrary Group, Ltd., ©Jeff Foott/Getty Images; **188** ©Purcell Team/Alamy Images; **218** (TL) Rubberball Productions; **219** (B) Getty Images, (BL) Hemera Technologies; **220** (TR) Hemera Technologies; **221** (TR) Rubberball Productions; **222** (BC) Getty Images; **223** (CR) ©Royalty-Free/Corbis, (B) Ghislain & Marie David de Lossy/Image Bank/Getty Images; **224** (BR) Getty Images; **225** (TR) Getty Images

High-Frequency Words

Identify and read the high-frequency words that you have learned. How many words can you read?

Unit R.1
a
green
I
see

Unit R.2
like
one
the
we

Unit R.3
do
look
was
yellow
you

Unit R.4
are
have
that
they
two

Unit R.5
he
is
three
to
with

Unit R.6
for
go
here
me
where

Unit 1.1
come
in
my
on
way

Unit 1.2
she
take
up
what

Unit 1.3
blue
from
get
help
little
use

Unit 1.4
eat
five
four

her
this
too

Unit 1.5
saw
small
tree
your

Unit 1.6
home
into
many
them

Unit 2.1
catch
good
no
put
said
want

Unit 2.2
be
could
horse
of
old
paper

Unit 2.3
live
out
people
who
work

Unit 2.4
down
inside
now
there
together

Unit 2.5
around
find
food
grow
under
water

Unit 2.6
also
family
new
other
some
their

High-Frequency Words

Unit 3.1
always
become
day
everything
nothing
stays
things

Unit 3.2
any
enough
ever
every
own
sure
were

Unit 3.3
away
car
friends
house
our
school
very

Unit 3.4
afraid
again
few
how
read
soon

Unit 3.5
done
know
push
visit
wait

Unit 3.6
before
does
good-bye
oh
right
won't

Unit 4.1
about
enjoy
give
surprise
worry
would

Unit 4.2
colors
draw
drew
great
over
show
sign

Unit 4.3
found
mouth

once
took
wild

Unit 4.4
above
eight
laugh
moon
touch

Unit 4.5
picture
remember
room
stood
thought

Unit 4.6
across
because
dance
only
opened
shoes
told

Unit 5.1
along
behind
eyes
never
pulling
toward

Unit 5.2
door
loved
should
wood

Unit 5.3
among
another
instead
none

Unit 5.4
against
goes
heavy
kinds
today

Unit 5.5
built
early
learn
science
through

Unit 5.6
answered
carry
different
poor